T0193660

Clearing of a Clouded Mind

To Yearn a Desire.
To Hope for Possibilities.
A Clear Sight, Beyond the Horizon

Casey Hardman

To order additional copies of this book, contact:
Xlibris
844-714-8691
www.Xlibris.com
Orders@Xlibris.com

ISBN: Softcover   978-1-6641-2447-9
               EBook   978-1-6641-2455-4

Print information available on the last page

Rev. date: 08/25/2020

When the mere thought of someone can create such bliss, it deserves recognition.
The purest form of happiness, is represented in your light.
Forever appreciation to you Matt M.

Contents

Dirty Little Secrets

A pen runs out, and the pages get full. What do we do when our mind isn't done? What
do we do when there's more to let out? Where do we go when it's not enough?
You can always find more room. You can always keep it within. In the end, you will always think…

What more could I have done? What more could I have said? The real
question to ask is, would it have even made a difference?

We all have something to say. We all have questions to ask ourselves, and to others. At
times we may not have the answers, nor do we receive them. It's whether or not we allow
those questions to rule over our actions, and to admit if we even need the answers.

To be afraid of what's to come. To not know what tomorrow will entail. For some
days, we not even care. To choose a battle of life and not accept defeat.

Who I am, and who I will become, has been a mystery. The path of finding that *someone* is what I can choose.
I choose to step out. Step out from darkness, step into the light, for what I see is my potential.

A Far Walk

I see the sun for what it does. The warmth it brings and the shine to aluminate.
With it, a meek tug into a vast world, with an endless dream.
Whether I'm cold, or in a shiver of worry, all I feel is the strength being given.
The heavens look down on me, shine a path, and what to do but follow.
There's no one around, there's no noise to distract. I am alone, yet happier than ever.
I see no clouds, I see no buildings. I hear no cars, and hear no voices.
All that is near is a constant field and no clouds to gloom.
I look around, although know it's only me, and I frolic.
No worry in mind, nothing to ground me. How can this be?

I stop at a flower. It's bright red petals catches my sight.
It's the only one I see in view. With all this field of just grass, where does it come from?
I then realize how I wanted colour, I wanted something bright to stand out.
I thought of beauty, and then the flower appeared.
Is this a dream where I can make the rules? Is this a world create in my image?

My clothes pure white, no pain I feel. No scars, no marks, not even tattoos.
All that I'm meant to be, is how I am right now.
The light that shines from above, guides me to which ever direction I choose.
If I go left, if I go right, it doesn't matter.
I'll always know, that which is above, will always be with me.
It will always watch over me wherever I walk.

Grace

Is it hate to just disgust.
Is it love to weed out the latched.
To walk a meadow and have the wind follow,
Is a feeling that allows all to soar above.

When the eyes are closed, the clouds surround.
You spread your wings, and can't see the ground.

Reality lost, calm you feel.
A tranquil mind, no need to heal.

Awaited Search

Time and time again, life poses many difficult situations.
Trying to find a smile, trying to find a pinch of ease,
We're left in wonder, in a void of uncertainty.
We gather all the strength we can find.
We lean on whatever we can hold onto.
When we think we've hit rock bottom,
When we believe we couldn't fall any further,
Where has the hope, the dream, the desire for better gone to?

Life poses many questions, wanting us to find the answers.
Life is an endless search with great possibilities.
Life can be hard and rough, but a search for peace,
A search of greatness and a smile,
A search of true friends,
A search of what makes us happiest,
Allows us to rest, find tranquility, and be ourselves.
With you, I can't imagine having to search any further.

Beauty Deep

How do we know when someone likes us?
A long gaze.
Puffy lips.
Soft glossy eyes?

When you see someone attractive, do you do something about it?
When the thought of them, crosses your mind,
Do you feel warmth?
Do you feel kindness?
Do you feel love?
At the very least, you should feel happy! No?

When the thought of them, is all you have.
It's because you miss them.
It's because you care.
It's because you know, just how truly great they are.
How much they mean to you!

Forward

The smell of a flower, awakens a memory.
The shiver of cold, hardens a desire.
To have once been, the gallows to your heart.
Burned in regret, I stayed and fret.
I saw a truth, that hid within.
The deeper you fell, the tighter my grip.

The pieces to mourn.
The pieces are torn.
The pieces are thrown.

A thought to send.
A thought to mend.
Our thought will blend.

Guilty Pleasures

Trying to change, trying to become something more.
Innocence penetrates a hardened passion.
Guilt hollows out the desire for purity,
And yet, the whore has surfaced.

To lay down, the feeling within.
To cover them, and walk away.
The eyes see, what it wants.
The eyes see, without a thought.
A movement swift, with fingers light.
A shiver creeps, throughout the body.

The whore to return.
The whore to reign.
The whore inside,
To reek havoc on temptations calmed.

Mistaken

The bitch has clawed it's way to return.
The damnation of ignorance is my bliss, and you get first kiss.
With time, the scar of you will be the giggle to my laugh.

I will sleep away this headache, that is created in your image.
I will wash away, all that is left from your touch.

A thought of change, made the mind forget.
Past mistakes, clouded in the glimmer of hope.
Spoken words with promises false.
Halted actions with hindered restraint.

Each time I'm here, each time I hear,
I've grown, I've changed.
I'm not the same.

How will I know, how can I know.
What is true, what's not the same.

My Saving Grace

Most people look up and see stars.
I look up and see you.
Where others consider royalty or those famous to be a hero...

I think of someone brave, pure of heart, and most generous.
I think of someone to inspire me for the gifts of humanity they possess.

When I think of my hero, it becomes a thought of light.
The brightness of one soul to fill my eyes. My mind. My heart.
To save me in even the darkest of days,
It is you! The saviour needed to find my grace.

A Day For You

Time goes on, and the seasons pass.
We learn and grow, and treasure the moments.
To those held dear, we never forget.

A constant joy you bring.
A constant smile upon your face.

To have a day, to call your own.
That's all I want. All I could hope for.

To follow your kindness.
To embody your presence.
To celebrate a life to share with others.

This Day To Us

We're born, we grow.
We eat, we sleep.
We laugh, we cry.
We dream, we hope.
We share, we hide.
We befriend, we Marry.
We hug, we kiss.
We're here, we're there.
We fight, we make up.
We drink, we celebrate.

We may do all of these things,
and I hope we do more.

They don't begin to describe the beauty,
created from our love.

The time we spend,
turned into endless memories to cherish.

Couldn't think of a better person to spend my days with.
You are my now, my before, and all that has yet to come.

Silence Drawn

I sit in silence, yet something is missing.
I go to the mall, yet never felt more alone.
I go to the gym, yet feel real weak.
I try to keep busy, yet my mind wanders.

Things haven't been the same.
Things haven't been as fun.
Things just haven't felt right.

I cannot feel warmth,
Without you by my side.

I cannot laugh at a joke,
Without your spoken words.

I cannot share a glance,
Without your caring eyes.

I'm void of you,
While left in your silence.

A Mother's Day

Many days throughout the year,
I wish for a day to just be yours.

For all that you've done,
And who you are.

Just one day is not enough.

Your gracious heart, warms any soul.
The thought of you, lights any day.

If one deserves the best...
If one deserves love...
If one deserves praise...

If one has the strength to never give up...
If one never asks for anything in return...

It would be you.

Because Of You

At peace I feel, because of you.
A smile that stays, because of you.
No longer a broken heart, because of you.
Have found hope, because of you.
Believing in words, because of you.

Because of you, I look forward to tomorrow.
Because of you, I have the desire to do better.
Because of you, I once again believe in others.
Because of you, my heart has healed.

Because of you,
I know what's right
I know what's true
I know what I want.

I know how it feels to be wanted,
Because of you!

An Unfound Search

I search, I go through numbers, and reach only but a dead end.
No one answers, and no new numbers left.
A constant check-in to your virtual life, yet no updates made.
I try to message, but no response is given.

Had we not been family, I'd be seen as a stalker.

To have been as close as we were.
To have grown up looking like twins.
To have often been judged as we have.
What now makes us the same?

A smile, a laugh, a giggle once shared.
No matter a cry, worry or fear.
A hug, a pat on the head.
The sympathy we once shared.

So easily spoken with,
Now not even a mention.

My Stride

A binding embrace enticed, yet unattainable.
I look around, left, not but alone.
In groups I'm left, to be their third.
In groups I stand, silent, and without a face.

With all that I do...
With all that I say...

To be the extra,
To be the side,
Is tiring.

It makes me weak.
It makes me vulnerable.

And so, I take a stance.
I take the leap, and with that,
This shall not be ME any longer.

Confusion

To define intention, yet act on instinct.
Can the action be held accountable,
Simply for the mere thoughtfulness?
The sincere pressure for security,
And a development for what is right.

A desire for that, which is out of reach.
The passion to never be acknowledged.
Truth is never precise, nor understanding.
Judgement is passed, and the thought is left with hope.
It's dissipated with an uninterested silence.

Afterlife Love

The whisper I hear, alerts my mind.
I look around, but I cannot find.
The chill that sweeps, the room around.
Creeps me out, with a familiar sound.

You've gone too soon,
You've left me alone.
Your days no more,
Your days I miss.

Quiet I sit, with an empty space.
No more smile, upon my face.
I cannot see you, cannot touch.
Left in tears, your picture to clutch.

You'll always be, in my heart.
You'll always have, all my love.
You'll always be, the one for me.
I'll always have, the memories we've made.

Becoming

We become the shadow, when that which we
hide from, darken who we are.

We become the lost, when the leading path
has no end.

We become the unspoken, when our words
have no meaning.

We become the not trusted, when our
truth is splintered.

We became the was, when no longer relevant.

Scribble

Fill me with hell. The cold that surrounds, need not freeze, for the wave to come will serve only but one purpose.

The arches of pain slowly tumble, and with every piece breaking off, an echo of the accident lingers.

To allow the fear to rule over.
To allow the pain to take over.
To hide and wallow, can it even be?
To undress and stand, what will it be?

That which lingers, becomes the was, and but a distant memory. In it's
place, sprouts the new, and what will be the great.

A fleeting truth is the bird to a cage. Unsure if it's meant to stay, or if it wants to go on it's
own path. We hope for a lasting stay, however, like all birds, it wants to flutter away.

To Wake On Christmas

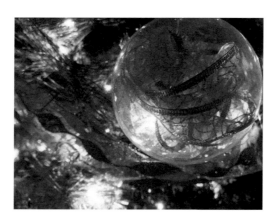

Contagious laughter, and endearing smile.
Warms through, even the most bitter of colds.
The end of a year, celebrated with joy.
To start anew, and past reflect.
The air around, freezes in white.
The colours of nature, buried in snow.
Lights go up, and twinkle through,
The early nights, and brighten spirits.
Warm the season, memories to make.
Awoken with love, on this festive morning.

Clear Away

Like stone I sit, eyes clear like glass.
Frozen I stay, with time to pass.
All around me, seems quick they move.
Headed a place, with something to prove.
I know I should. I know I must.
Get up and go, like in a gust.
Can't seem to think, no thought in mind.
I dare not talk, and you'll think I'm blind.
So stunned by sad, hit hard with quiet.
To again smile, to again I'll try it.

Shine On Me

What is light but a guide in the impending darkness.
Thoughts of doubt may fill our heads,
But never give up. Never allow the hatred voice to win.

Sometimes, the best way to move on without sadness,
Is to remove the reminders of once was.

Forgiveness doesn't mean you must forget.
It's knowing the importance of one's existence,
While allowing a chance to learn and grow.

Insecurities will remain,
When one chooses not to stand up.
When one chooses not to try for themselves.
Look within yourself, and then the light within,
Will shine upon your brightness.

Deep Within

To think of those that inspire, it isn't the hope to become a version of them.
It is the hope to become a better version of oneself.
Use their success to show you how possible it can be.

Whether your success is as great as theirs,
It shouldn't matter, because it will become yours, and yours alone.

It's having rough and bad days that make you appreciate the smaller,
and good things about everyday life.
It gives you the opportunity to strengthen your mind, test your patience,
and will build up your self confidence.

The only thing that will prevent this,
is to be closed off to the possibility that you can get through it.
You are the strongest ally you have!

13 Years Too Much Conclusion:

Years of memories, saddened my mind.
The struggle for hope, left me blind.
A life with pain, was to live a life in fear.
Nothing to gain, until I allowed it to clear.
To accept the was, and start anew.
Forgive mistakes, was all I knew.
My pages filled, I thought I was done.
To my surprise, I hadn't even begun.
A smile once lost, regained it's place.
With enough time, it came back to my face.
Emotions calmed, was able to breathe.
Strength I found, was buried beneath.
To stride away, from my tears of sorrow.
Allows me to look, forward to tomorrow.

Your Heart

No matter how much, or how little time goes by,
You are always on my mind, and in my heart!
No matter the mood, whether full of cheer or sadness,
My love for you stays strong!
No matter the day, if it lingers or speeds on by,
I'm at a standstill thinking of you!

Your kindness can never be matched.
Your love can never falter.
Your hope can never wither.
Your passion can only be shared.

You are an exception to rules, for you're one of a kind.
You hold within, something only others can dream of.
You're the blessing in disguise, allowing others to feel.
Your strength is real, and it spreads around you.

With you, I feel.
With you, I see the light.
With you, I'm never cold.
With you, I'm free.

Thanks to you, I see the beauty.
Thanks to you, I know no pain.
Thanks to you, I know true love.

Belief

One does not simply stop growing.
Day to day experiences, enable unpredicted growth from within.
The change surrounding the people, events, and things in ones life,
is the difference that may be needed to add new perspectives.
Taking a step back at times, might just be what is truly needed,
in order to get yourself even further ahead.

Some days it's okay to feel like a piece of crap.
So long as you remind yourself why you actually aren't.
There's always a reason and way to prove why you aren't.
It just becomes a matter of staying strong, while finding patience.

Never stop believing!
The belief you have in yourself,
can be the very thing that will allow you,
your best chance to succeed.

Life's Friend

Life introduces you to many great things.
Friends and shopping, even a sunburn that stings.
We go through the days, with giggles and tears.
The love for others, strips away all fears.

Your kindness shines, brighter than a star.
Your laughter warms, even when at afar.

Words can't express, who you are to me.
Couldn't forget, what you allow me to see.

A true friend, while always being there.
You've always shown, how much you care.

Heart Slain

The day too short, with time wasted in thought.
I try not to think, how you've been caught.

To be who you are, is all that I ask.
To be true to your heart, is your next task.

The laughs that we've had, our touch to embrace.
Has hidden feelings, while warming my face.

To sit in silence, with time standing still.
Muster a memory, while feeling the thrill.

A growing distance, to test us true.
My heart you took, leaving it slew.

Our love created, the moments we share.
Come this time, did you ever care.

To Look Above

I look up, and the sun's gone down.
The stars are trying to pierce through the smoke.
All around, the city ablaze.
All around, the sirens strike.

I look up, and my body is left numb.
Standing still, with my eyes fixed ahead.
The tree in front, beams with light.
The tree in front, clears the mind.

I look up, and my mind's forgotten.
The world around, fades into never ending night.
My tears to stream, from those fallen in hate.
My tears to stream, from what needs to change.

Cray Cray

Where to hide,
My creeping stride.
I quietly glide,
Upon bushes wide.
Not yet lied.
I mustn't slide,
Down the side,
Into high tide.
Do I confide,
Within my pride.
Become the bride,
Means I tried.
If I'm fried,
Ends with genocide.

Just Love Me

I breathe to live,
But live to love.
I climb to fall,
But fall to rise.
I look to see,
But see to feel.
I speak to touch,
But touch to listen.
I smile to hide,
But hide to forget.
I drink to leave,
But leave to cry.
I stay to remember,
But remember to forgive.
I laugh to learn,
But learn to care.
I grow to help,
But help to breathe.

Enough Time

Attention needed,
Feelings pleaded.
Time so cruel,
Now the fool.
Loose restraint,
Time to faint.
A random glance,
Ends my stance.
A new desire,
Ends with fire.

A look despair,
Can never be fair.
Feel the burn,
But wait your turn.
If you wait,
And save this date,
Cries to stop,
When bodies drop.

The past becomes the now.
No reason to feel wow.
It's time to fix,
It's time we mix.
It's time to mend,
About time we blend.

Heated Air

I try to slumber, but my eyes won't close.
The air so thick, my limbs fall numb.
An area moved, where the touch is cool.
A brief relief, refreshing and absorbed.

I try to rest, but tears turn to sweat.
Gamble is the wind, while hope is a breeze.
I move in patience, where less is more.
Unwrap, uncover, undress to lay.

I try to sleep, when my eyes fall heavy.
A piercing rise, which fills the room.
The desire to freeze, becomes too real.
Feeling boiled and burned, when will it end.

The Cold In Christmas

The air is cold, and the days seem short.
No flowers bloomed, and the trees are bare.
The ground we walk on, frozen in ice.
Animals to roam, have gone to sleep.
The season we're in, sounds depressing.
But to open your eyes, and the beauty you'll see.
Nature is frozen…

To heal. To grow. To blossom that much more.
A negative temperature, to bring in the snow.
Covers the ground, the trees, and plants.

A season to water, and freeze the beauty.
The children's laughter, while they frolic in glee.
A man they make, out of snow to smile.
Good things to come, from the cold that strikes.
Lights and jingles, reefs and stockings…

Decorate the house, while singing as one.
A family we are, to celebrate the joy.
A tree goes up, and Saint Nick appears.
Be safe and well, smile and cheer.
Remember the good, and that Christmas is here.

2 Years

2 years ago,
I was alone, thinking I was unable to find love.
After months of staying home
alone, I decided to go out.
After months of feeling alone, I took a chance.

At first, I didn't want to talk to anyone.
At first, I just wanted to go home.
At first, I never paid attention to anyone,
Including you.

You spoke with kindness and sincerity.
You couldn't be real.
You couldn't be true.
You saved me from myself.

2 years ago, we took a chance.
Uncertain of what to come, what to expect.
Unsure was our beginning, being long and tough.
We had hope.

We gained each other.
We fell in love.

2 Years gone by…
I gained a smile.
I gained a home, a family.
I gained hope, a dream, and love!

2 Years gone by…
I've never been happier.
I've never been more in love.
I've never been so hopeful.
I've never been so grateful.

2 Years From Now,
All I want,
All I see,
All I need,
IS YOU!

Pass of The Shadow

With every shadow, there is a watchful eye.
To recall or not, whether a movement has passed.

With every flickering light, there is a racing heart.
A growing thump within, ignites a worried thought.

With every creak of noise, there is a lingering presence.
To be alone, becomes a question unanswered.

Around every corner, not knowing what to expect.
To stand at the ready, trying to look around.

Every time a light turns off, not knowing what's in the dark.
To peep around, and wonder if you're not alone.

Close your eyes, and you allow them the chance.
To see what cannot be seen, is it really there?

They get to you, when you least expect.
The horror in the shadow, which pounces quick.

Transference

You work so hard.
Your mind stays true.
Never doubt, never gave in.
It'll all work out.
It'll all feel right.

Be your best.
Be the light.
Be the smile,
To bring you through.

Don't dim your mind.
Don't darken your spirit.
Do what you can,

And you'll see it's enough.

Each day I rise.
Each day I fall.
You are there,
And everything is fine.

From 2 to 4.
From 4 to Now.
It's times like these,
I'm proud to know.
My place with you,
Will forever grow.

Where's My Puppy

A puppy I want.

From the beginning, to be in it's wake.
From the beginning, to bless it a name.
From the beginning, first steps it takes.
A puppy I want.

To watch it grow, tricks to teach.
To watch it grow, comfort to share.
To watch it grow, to cuddle with care.
A puppy I want.

Become best friends, take a walk in the park.
Become best friends, stay up after dark.
Become best friends, we'll train your bark.
A dog I need.

You'll grow with love, and never judge.
You'll grow in style, and need not want.
You'll grow and prosper, a promise from me.

Easy Am I

Easily cut down,
and then I bleed.

Easily thrown aside,
and so I linger.

Easily ignored,
and yet I stay.

Easily mislead,
I'm left to wonder.

Easily felt used,
but continue to give.

Easily being misheard,
so I search for words.

Easily not believed,
but I continue to try.

Easily taken advantage of,
why do I not go.

Easily able to forgive,
I hide away the tear.
Easily broken apart,
no one to pick up the pieces.

Easily feeling unloved,
while my whole heart is given.

So easily forgotten,
so easily I vanish.

After Thought

I do what I can, not make a fuss.
Swallow my pride, and ride the bus.
I search for ways, hope for a clue.
Stressed to the bone, left with the flu.
I walk then stumble, my head to shake.
A daze I'm in, I must not forsake.
Eyes with bags, in need of sleep.
Squint to see, a need so deep.
Avoid the hustle, but slow to move.
Lift up my head, something to prove.
No one can see, no one must know.
The pain within, I must continue to glow.
So weak I feel, but I must fight.
Others in need, must strengthen my might.
To go ahead, give all I got.
Feel assured, I would have fought.
In memory lane, never made it there.
With so much hope, never quite fair.
Died on the way, saddened my heart.
Know I tried, wash clean your heart.

An Ice-Cream Walk

Sun is out, feeling hot.
Cool me off, don't wanna rot.
So sweet a treat.
So cold to eat.
Sugar galore.
I want more.
Flavours aplenty.
My tummy's empty.
Toppings to scatter.
Don't care if I'm fatter.
Short or long, line to wait.
Much fun to have, on our date.
New tubs each day.
New smiles that stay.
Try me now, try those then.
Cone or bowl, a choice of when.

Your Face I See

I lay in our bed, and all I can see is you.
While deciding to get up, I turn and watch you sleep.
Your eyes are closed, and you don't move.
I'm left to wonder, what dreams you're having.
So peaceful you look. So relaxed you seem.
I lay looking at you, and all I can do is smile.
Not to be creepy. Not to be weird.
I smile at you, while flashes appear.
A joke you told. A door you opened.
Each day we spent, my heart had grown.
I keep to my side. Don't want to move.
I lay in my bed, holding the covers.
Looking at your pillow, I see the indent from your head.
I reach out with my hand, but don't want to ruin it.
My clutch on the covers tighten.
From the smell of once was, triggers my tears.
They wash away what I want to see.

While I lay in my bed, all I want to see is you.
I look over, and your side untouched.
Your side remains. Your indent stays.
I reach out, as if you're there asleep.
I cry out, for you to return.
A smile you gave me. The memory to cherish.
I'm broken with cries. Your passing stuns me.
To wish you here. To watch you sleep.
So simple. So small a desire.
You grew my heart. I smiled for you.
Now here I lay. Alone, not wanting to move.
Seeing your face, upon the pillow beside me.
When you passed, my heart you tore.
My heart in pieces. Can never be fixed.
All along, you had my heart. My love.
Broken now, forever my heart will remain.

Worry Not The Question

The day crept up, and I'm stricken with fear.
Drawn from the unknowing, the day itself not.
Gathered thoughts created from possibilities.
Molding themselves together, growing beyond imaginative.

Questions plundered the inner core.
Answers become vacant, leaving room for more.
Thought to bring a smile, brought worry in it's place.
A day of vibrance, replaced by self destruction.

To take a step back, to clear the mind.
The purpose of doing, to heal with intent.
Remembrance of why, and to whom the observer.
Never was for them, but for thee told true.

Solace granted, from the story you've written.
Ignorance of the negative, that plagues your way.
Lift up your worth, held high to stand.
Others cannot, define your strength.

Embrace your beauty, embody the resilience.
The questions that strike, worry not of them.

Voided Presence

I stayed over time
I forgave the pain
I took the blame
I then became blind

You see what you want
You hear what you need
You speak without knowing
You leave to be ahead

Do you know who you are?
Do you know what you want?

Do you still have pain?
Do you need to be set free?

What was your reason
What truth stays within
What couldn't be said
What do I not know

I thought I was there
I tried to care
I didn't mean to judge
I only meant to show love

What's To Come

Curious is the mind. Creative thoughts to share, with worlds to explore. The transition from mind to pen, allows detail to description, to translation. To begin in brief, with small clouds of ideas. With time and thought, they grow, they expand, and begin to live inside the creator.

What was once a mere dream, now, becomes a story. There is body. There is length. The detail is there, with expansions creating it's own world. From pen to paper, one mind to another, it is passed. It needs just one other to become real.

To look ahead, there is no time. Nothing is set in stone. To form the thought to idea, leading to fruition, requires ease, and no clock. Patience is at the front, leading the way. It paves the road to it's goal.

Each world becomes a milestone. When one is finished, it never disappears. A door is open, that leads the creative mind to other possibilities. Another thought. Another dream. Another idea is formed, with much to share. Always more to share. More to create. To look ahead, there's always more to come.

The Intent For Apology

Apologies can only start by saying sorry while actually meaning it! To say "sorry", it doesn't mean forgiveness needs to be met, nor does it mean for things to start going back to how they were. Saying sorry just means there is a deep sadness built with regret for something said with an intention of hurt.

Regardless of how felt, hurt or otherwise, for something said, feeling
shameful for the words is a desire for apology.

There isn't an intention to regain what was, but to try and make amends with a hope for peace.
Feeling attacked while being confused, drew the question of what to say or how to react.

It has always been a hope in it's purest form, to witness you gain love, calmness, and the best of life. Having such a strong hope, disabled the mind to know mistakes may be made. Such a high standard is questionable and unrealistic. After having witnessed the results of what mistakes could lead to, it draws on the fear of repeating them. It becomes the hope to help as much as possible, to keep it away, as it isn't something desired.

Mistakes can and will be made. It becomes up to oneself to see them, recognize, and act accordingly. It is up to oneself if it is not in the best interest. It is not up to an outside observer to point them out. It is not up to an outside observer to decide if it is even a mistake.

Wherever things end up, whatever path is chosen, there will forever be an entanglement. It becomes a choice to remember the smiles, the laughs, and not the pressures of life. The path has lead so far, while enduring too much. That accomplishment can never be demolished, not from anyone. Hope for a deserved life is what will remain in me for you.

You be you, and stay true to yourself. I know that to be the most beautiful of souls.

A Tale of Too Many Lies

The eyes see the truth. The mind decides the reality of the observer. The heart feels all connection to the soul. With changing any one of these by choice, is to justify a personal mean of change. A lie no less. We lie to hide what's within. What we choose is not acceptable to an outside viewer. We lie to satisfy the hunger of those in need of a place, of a passion, and of a personal vendetta.

Where do we draw the line of creating a false reality, a better reality to our liking? When have we gone too far in our new identity, that wouldn't allow anyone to truly know us? Knowledge of what is real, what is right, is merely a bleak turn of truth, but the path of return may never be just.

When we tell one lie, our mind creates a bump in our thoughts. That bump represents a moment in our life that we must never forget. That bump is the thing that we have to continually feed in order to maintain its existence. In other words, we must keep that lie alive by accepting it, by acknowledging it, by remembering it so it doesn't get caught. One lie is never just that; One lie. It always grows, becoming more than just one. It becomes hungry for more. It begins needing additional lies piled on, to keep itself around.

Is it too much? Does it become too much to handle? Are you able to remember what was said, what was thought to be? Avoidance of others in conversation is what takes over, as the spoken word has no truth. It has no meaning. Your belief hangs with flaws as it tries to grasp what is true. Until the release of that first lie, like dominos there will forever be standing gaps.

The Path

It's 11pm; My body is relaxed laying underneath my plaid sheets and a dark coffee brown comforter. My eyes are closed, not tight, but to the point where it should be easy to fall asleep. I'm wearing red briefs, a white muscle shirt, and obviously no socks. I hate when you see those people who wear socks to bed. I mean, you're about to fall asleep, why hide any smells they may have, and if they're ugly, no one will see them anyways. I brushed my teeth for the second time today. I skipped flossing. I didn't feel as though it mattered since yet again, I'm sleeping by myself. My hands and face are cleansed, and moisturized. I took a sleep aid, now why can't I fall asleep?

This question tends to fill my head most nights. I do everything right before having to sleep, and yet nothing. Some nights I wonder if it's because I didn't floss, and this is my body's way of telling me I'm not quite ready to turn in. Please! My body and mind aren't that smart, trust me! It never dawned on me until right now, this night.

I've never been a fan of music; I will rarely put on the radio station just to have something on in the background, or even to dance to. The only time I listen to music is if I'm in a friend's car, and they decide to put on their playlist, or if I'm in a bar. I find music to be an unnecessary excuse for noise. I would much prefer to sit on my couch quietly with a glass of cheap wine. I can't afford anything good, and anything on the best sellers list. My apartment is always so quiet, which is the way I prefer it. Even with all of the quiet I surround myself with, why can't I turn off the noises in my head?

I live modernly; Glass tables with black frames. A lot of items made of browns, blacks, and of course beige. This stupid neighbour of mine I think is a night-owl. I've never seen him leave during the day, and every night he has people over. If someone wants to have a social life, by all means go for it, but I need my quiet. I need my sleep. Why must my neighbour keep me up, with his loud and cheerful friends. Don't they sleep? Don't they work during the day?

Where do I go? Where can I find what I'm looking for? What must I do to find peace within my mind? My eyes are left wide open, scanning the room. I try to see past the shadows. I try to look through the noise, at the still and quiet walls. Photos hung, with shelves sporadic. I scan my items, to pass the time. I await my eyes to feel heavy, so they will want to close. What must happen, before I drift away?

Purity Of Deceit

What is the untold story of emotions and how they've come to be. What exactly they are. More importantly what kind of creation they are.

In a world of the untold and complete fantasy, all emotions are an entity of beings that form the human soul. Each emotion has been around since the dawn of time. They have been around in every world, in every dimension known to the galaxy to create a new meaning to life. In retrospect, they are the exact definition of life. Or so, that is what *they* believe.

For eons they have been fighting with the Gods to be the ruler of existence. The Gods created man, but they needed something more for their creation, and so they called upon the Emotions to give the beings meaning. The Emotions agreed to this request, but in secret decided to one day disobey. One day they would try and claim the world which we call Earth.

As time went on, the people of the Gods began to lose faith, and with this, came an opportunity. There is no greater power than the belief from those we give life. With havoc wreaking in the heavens, the Emotions take a stand and place themselves on Earth to take back what they feel is truly theirs... The acknowledgement from the humans, and to have all know who their true "Gods" are. And so, the battle begins, but who will prevail...

Isolation

When does it become too much? To ask a question, with not knowing the answer, becomes a worry to the mind. To live a life with only questions and never the answer, became my way to pass each day. To try and hide myself from the world of confusion, became an escape to that which troubles me.

Should I not witness what goes on around me, allowing me to have hope. If I do not engage with others, I cannot judge. With blinding my eyes, I am left seeing what I deem acceptable.

I am left wondering if my choice to venture on my own is a decision just. After much danger and trouble surfacing, should I not want to seek care and shelter?

Time is the only thing that can't find it's way back. Once passed, one must do what they can to ensure the remaining amount is viewed with clarity. Time becomes sacred. It becomes counted with precision. Time became my crutch.

Spark of The Rainbow

One person's existence is not the same as any other. Differences in appearance, speech, attire, personal relationships, should differentiate from others. Why should we all be the same. What is the point from looking alike, speaking alike, acting alike. Who are we, if we are just another copy of each other.

There are an abundance of ways we as people can show our individuality. Some examples come from forms that are out of our control, and those reasonings should be the ones to celebrate most. We are born into the universe without cause, without being able to pick and choose anything. We are who we are! How can it be considered fair for another to judge and ridicule based on something out of reach to our control?

Why is it acceptable to assume one life is greater than another? That was a rhetorical question. The answer is simple… All life should be considered as great as others. We are equals, as we are all born the same. We are all without choice. We are all slated life to be lived in our chosen eyes, with limitations.

Some things like love, race, gender, bodily structure, facial appearance; are things given to allow difference. To allow individuality. Why must one choose hate for any of those because they differ from their own. Not only should they be accepted, but, they need to be celebrated.

To open your eyes, and see beauty in the world, is to find acceptance in others. Ignite the bright, and share your pride. Wear it strong, and rise with acceptance.

The Tree of Dreams

To look upon a tree, while being filled with dreams, is to have a tree full of worlds.

As I clinch the brown leather arms rests with a tight grip, I'm left in silence. It's been ten years since I was last here. It's been ten years since I was asked to relive that day. Ten years since the sorrow and pain filled my thoughts, draining through my eyes. It's been ten years since the thought of losing them made me cry uncontrollably.

For ten years I have been left in a constant nightmare, unsure if I would wake up. No child should have to have seen what I did. No child should be left alone as I have been. No child should have to watch both of their parents taken right in front of them. No child should have to cradle and hold both of their taken parents, while screaming in pain until someone came to save them.

What started as a day filled with laughter and joy, ended with only pain and bloodshed. Never understood it. I don't think I ever could. How one person could strip away another's smile and love, is a concept I don't want to know. Why one person would want to cause so much grief to another, is a reason I could never understand.

What am I left to do when my reason for life has been take away. What can I do but dream of what could have been, had that horrified day not have happened. Who will I become without the guidance from those who gave me life. What kind of world will I choose to live in.

A Bakers Read

The air is sweet, and the counters are powdered.
A description brief, but the measurements exact.
Ingredients range, depending on the meal.
The tools I use, laid out and washed.

A pin to roll, and a finger to pinch.
An eye to level, so better not flinch.
An oven heated, and beeps when ready.
Grab your trays, and keep yourself steady.

Time for shopping, and time for prep.
Time for mixing, and time to cook.
So much needed, so time yourself out.

Soft and chewy, or crumbly and crunchy.

Fruit or bran, chocolate or raisins.
How do you choose, when all so good.
Over cook, and they're hard as wood.

To know one's limits,
To watch for allergies,
To count the calories.

To keep within, your diet restrictions.
To hope you don't need, another prescription.

Now grab an apron, grab your cheer.
Grab a glass, and pour your beer.
There's fun to be had, laughs to be made,
Memories to share, and recipes to be slayed.

End Of The Storm

My body stands, frozen from worry.
Darkness clouds, with no dimmer of power.
Screams I hear
Cries I feel
Fear I dread

In front of my window, left to wonder.
How is this happening, can it be real.
The thunder roars
The lightening strikes
The fires ignite

Do I stay, and cower inside.
Should I chance, break free from here.
A picture falls
A shadow nears
Instinct kicks in

I dash away
Refuse to stay
In dark I run
I miss the sun
Screams all around
Another soul I found

A child left alone, he sits to cry.
How can I run past, not even try.
I stop to help, and to lend a smile.
That's all it took, ending this inner trial.

To give a smile, with open eyes,
To trust a soul, will warm your heart.
The darkness that clouds, can end with time.
Believe in yourself, and the light will appear.
For fear to leave, relax the mind.
Find the hope, that resides within.

Printed in the United States
By Bookmasters